THE 30 MINUTE PATENT MBA

FOR STARTUP CEOS & CTOS

JAMES BILLMAIER

TURBOPATENT

v 1.6

CONTENTS

INTRODUCTION

This mini-book is **NOT** intended for lawyers. It is for business leaders, technologists, and/or entrepreneurs working in early-stage startups to midsize businesses—basically any company that does not have a dedicated Intellectual Property (IP) staff and a multi-million dollar IP budget. If you are a business leader in a company with the resources to have dedicated patent staff, you should read *Inventioneering* by James Billmaier and Britt Griffith, which offers strategies to help U.S. companies win on the global intellectual property front.

The purpose of *The Patent MBA* is to quickly—and in plain English—convey the necessary information to early-stage company leaders. Why? Because heretofore the topic of patents has been taught as an overwhelming complicated legal matter. As a result, business executives often de-prioritized obtaining patent knowledge, instead devoting their time and budget solely to the development of their product or service. If they do embark on an intellectual property business strategy, it's most often relegated to legal experts with little grounding in the product or business. In reality, invention, and the protection thereof, should be well understood—and embraced—by business leaders, and must be integrated throughout their company's product development and business operations. Patents are indeed technical and legal documents. However, patents are first and foremost a business tool and strategic asset. Patent knowledge is no longer optional for anyone attempting to build a valuable business.

As Shane Wall, Chief Technology Officer and Global Head of HP Labs, said:

> "When considering a partnership or acquisition of a company, it is assumed that they have properly protected their inventions...that is a big reason we are interested in them."

A strategy to build value and achieve a competitive advantage that does not include the protection of the company's inventions is the approach of amateurs.

Sustainable business success comes from a combination of things: It comes from delivering a compelling product or service that allows you to capture initial market share. It comes from understanding and reacting to continual market and technological shifts. And, finally, it comes from defending your company's gains by erecting barriers to market entry from competitors.

This short book is designed to quickly provide you with the practical data and details necessary to enable the affordable creation of a twenty-first-century patent strategy for your business.

WHY BOTHER WITH PATENTS?

11 REASONS YOU SHOULD CARE ABOUT PATENTS

1. Data-proven substantial increase in likelihood of receiving funding
2. Data-proven substantial increase in funding valuations and exit valuations
3. Data-proven substantial increase in likelihood of successful exit
4. Protection during discussions with investors, partners, and acquirers
5. Competitive advantage vs. copycats and fast followers
6. Serves as trade currency in IP assertion matters against your company
7. Stronger position in acquisition negotiations
8. Establishing "Patent Pending" or "Patented" for stronger market positioning
9. Patent process results in a superior product definition and value proposition
10. Demonstrates professionalism of management team
11. Team motivation

Let's go into each of these in a little more detail.

Data-proven substantial increase in likelihood of receiving funding

As an early-stage company your odds of obtaining first-round funding increases by 53% if you have invested in patents vs. early-stage companies without evidence of a patent strategy. With investment in a patent portfolio your odds of receiving funding in the second round are further increased by 67% over early-stage companies that did not use part of their first-round funding to create an IP advantage.

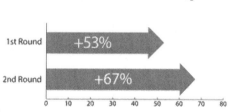

Patents Increase Likelihood of Funding

Source: Office of Chief Economist Report

Data-proven substantial increase in funding valuations and exit valuations

As an early-stage company your valuation at the first round of funding increases by 23% if you have invested in patents vs. early stage companies without evidence of a patent strategy. With investment in a patent portfolio your average valuation in the second round is further increased by 29% over early-stage companies that did not use a portion of their first-round funding to create an IP advantage.

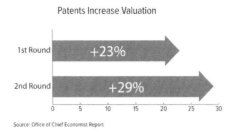

Patents Increase Valuation

Source: Office of Chief Economist Report

Data-proven substantial increase in likelihood of successful exit

As an early-stage company with a patent portfolio, your likelihood of a successful exit in the form of an acquisition increases by 83% vs. early stage companies without a patent portfolio. And your company's odds of achieving an initial public offering (IPO) vs. a company without patents is increased by 153%.

Protection during discussions with investors, partners, and acquirers

In a perfect world, a startup CEO would be able to count on the protection provided by a nondisclosure agreement (NDA) for meetings with potential investors, partners, and acquirers. But the fact is that most potential investors won't sign NDAs, leaving the startup disclosing its "secret sauce" without any protection. Filing provisional patent applications on core ideas prior to disclosing ideas to potential investors allows the savvy startup CEO to protect his or her company value proactively, without relying on VCs to keep the startup's plans under wraps.Remember, those VCs meet with hundreds of entrepreneurs every year.

Potential partners and acquirers are almost always larger and more powerful than your company. So they usually get to decide what the nondisclosure agreement contains. All too often, these NDAs leave little real protection against these organizations who learn from your meeting only to create or enhance their own internal developments. Ever hear of a residual clause? Filing and prosecuting patent applications on the inventive technology that gives your company market differentiation and competitive advantage will give these organizations pause before they set about ripping off your ideas. It will also provide you with a path to recourse should they decide to do so.

Competitive advantage vs. copy-cats and fast followers

The instant your company files a provisional or non-provisional patent application, it can begin to mark the related products and services "PATENT PENDING." This simple mark gives copycats pause. China's government is now taking patent infringement much more seriously. Those Chinese or other offshore companies whose sole business is to make cheaper versions of the designs of others will more likely avoid copying, manufacturing, and distributing a patented or patent-pending product vs. a non-protected product.

Serves as trade currency in IP assertion matters against your company

As an early-stage or medium-sized company, one of the inherent advantages you enjoy vs. large entities is speed. However, large companies can use patent infringement assertion as a way to slow down or stop your company. If you have no patent assets, you have little trade currency with which to barter. With a well-built patent portfolio, you are actually in an interestingly strong position compared to large corporations. An injunction (stopping a company from shipping one of its products due to infringement of your IP) is far more financially damaging to a public company whose shareholder satisfaction is directly tied to the company's financial results.

Stronger negotiating position in acquisition negotiations

I have seen a startup acquisition discussion go from the withdrawal of an offer to a completed deal of over $300 million. This occurred during an M&A evaluation where the large company's engineering team concluded and reported to its management that it could rebuild the same solution in six months for approximately $1 million.

While this is an extreme case, it is common for another party, once it has deeply studied your product or service, to conclude that it could rebuild it far cheaper than it cost you to create it. The truth is that you could probably rebuild your own technology at a fraction of the cost that was required the first time.

The happy ending to this story is that the startup company had patented its key inventions, making it not only legally dangerous for the large company to simply copy the technology, but also impractical to work around the patents. As a result, the large company consummated an acquisition of the startup for $300 million!

Establishing "Patent Pending" or "Patented" for stronger market positioning

We have discussed how "Patented" or "Patent Pending" helps slow or stop fast followers from ripping off your special sauce. In addition, a patent mark sends a signal to the marketplace that you and your team have brought something special to the market—something different and better than competitive products.

Patent process results in a superior product definition and value proposition

Common questions asked in the process of creating IP around your company's product or service are: "Why is your product/service better than what is in the market today?" And "What would your sales or marketing team say to potential customers as to why they should spend their time and money on your product or service as opposed to your competition's?"

Most startups have a notion of the answers to these questions but often cannot state it in a clear and succinct fashion. Companies often spend tens of thousands or hundreds of thousands of dollars on consultants to help them create well-thought-out plans and messages to describe those plans. Startup companies that don't have a rock-solid handle on their vision of their market differentiation will waste huge sums of money and misdirected company effort in product development and marketing.

The patent process forces deep thought and documentation on what is different and better about what your company is attempting to build. This is far cheaper than bringing in a marketing consultant, not to mention the wasted effort inherent in trying to decipher a hazy vision. Avoiding both are unintended upsides of working through the patent process early on. Even more, once that patent process is completed, your company not only has a very clear idea of its special sauce, it also has the legal means to protect that special sauce in the marketplace.

Demonstrates professionalism of management team

Patent applications are impressive documents. They contain specifications for how the special sauce can be developed, as well as drawings and other figures that express detailed thoughts and plans. Smart investors conduct a thorough assessment of how your engineering processes and methods are performed; they take a deep dive into your go-to-market plans and business model, etc. The smartest investors—and you do want the smartest money backing your company—investigate your company's competitive advantage, including protecting your company's most valuable inventions. This does not entail just studying a patent application or two that you may have in process, but rather the continual, repeatable and sustainable process and culture of protecting your company's IP assets. Amateur founders and company executives deal with this in an ad-hoc manner, whereas professionals practice a disciplined approach to patents and trade secrets.

Team motivation

Being a named inventor on a granted patent brings a sense of pride. Patents allow members of your team to build demonstrable value in their careers and can be combined with simple and inexpensive invention reward programs that enhance employee satisfaction (specifics on reward programs addressed later). Establishing a culture of invention early on in your company's development increases both the flow of innovation within your team and the value of your venture.

2

WHY DON'T ALL STARTUPS PATENT THEIR INVENTIONS?

Clearly, there are overwhelming advantages to obtaining patents and trade secrets. Despite this, many startup CEOs and management teams do not make it a priority to protect their businesses' most vital assets. Here are some of the (mostly bad) reasons we frequently hear:

- It is too expensive
- We don't have the time
- We thought software isn't patentable
- We don't want our competitors to see what we are doing
- Members of our team don't believe in patents
- We use open source software
- Patents have no value for startups because we can't afford to enforce them
- I don't think we have any protectable IP

It is too expensive

This is the most frequent reason given for not pursuing patents, an argument not without merit given that startups are always resource-constrained. Cash is precious, and the company's existence is often predicated on a CEO's ability to make those dollars stretch as far as possible. Executive teams are offered the false choice of either developing their product and market or legally protecting their innovations. This is true only because the traditional law firm costs for drafting and prosecuting patent applications do not fit with lean startup budgetary constraints. Many firms still charge via billable hours, shifting the risk onto the client and making it difficult to plan expenses.

Additionally, organizational structures employed by most law firms are bloated and horrendously inefficient—costs that are passed on to the client. Modern, smarter patent approaches leverage technology and deliver patents efficiently while increasing quality. This allows forward-thinking patent professionals to employ affordable, fixed-fee structures, which allow early-stage companies to both develop their product/service AND protect their intellectual property.

We don't have the time

Time is another resource that is heavily constrained in a startup. Small teams juggle titanic amounts of work, so adding one more item to the to-do list of an already over-taxed engineering team seems like a fool's errand. In reality, the patenting process should be an integral part of the engineering process. Further, much of the documentation an engineering team already prepares in its regular work process is actually highly useful in preparing a patent application, and having a patent helps to ensure that products developed by the engineering team are not wasted effort.

We thought software isn't patentable

The court decision in *Alice Corp. v CLS Bank* led to wild speculation that software might not be patentable. However, successive court decisions have reaffirmed the patentability of software, and computer-related patents continue to be a huge percentage of the patent office's total volume of work. Your competition understands that software innovation is very patentable.

If we disclose our secret sauce our competitors will just change something minor and copy us

People are sometimes concerned that when a patent application is filed, it will be made public and allow competitors to see what is being done. However, if the application is not going to be filed in multiple countries, an applicant may request that the application remain unpublished until it is granted.

Even if you do wish to file your patent application in countries beyond the United States, a provisional patent application is only published in conjunction with the publishing of a non-provisional patent. This process will provide about two-and-a-half years of complete confidentiality of your filed applications, which is usually long enough to create and then begin marketing your product or service.

I don't believe in patenting and am philosophically opposed to it

Remember, just because you are a conscientious objector to the patent system doesn't mean you aren't a target. Regardless of whether or not a person believes in gravity, a fall from an airplane without a parachute will very likely result in serious injury or death. Further, just because a CEO is philosophically opposed to creating proprietary value does not absolve him or her of the duty to employees and shareholders to protect the company's assets and value.

We use open source software as the basis for our product

Despite what some people believe, open source and patenting are not mutually exclusive. Many companies that use open source software and build value on top of it create patentable material on top of the publicly shared code. Red Hat, a leading producer of open source software, reportedly has more than 10 issued patents, and 163 pending patent applications in the U.S. alone.

In its "Patent Promise," Red Hat has stated its opposition to the philosophy of patents, yet acknowledges their necessity in the current system, and pragmatically uses patents as a shield against their competitors.

Patents aren't valuable because a startup company can't enforce them

Patents are valuable regardless of the size of the company, and are likely even more valuable to a smaller company. Having strong IP increases the likelihood of success in litigation, and the stronger the likelihood of success, the more likely it is that there will be a respected law firm willing to take the case on a no-upfront-payment success-based model. In fact, there are funds set up that finance the cost of a solid patent case and only collect if the case succeeds.

It is a common misconception that just because you "aren't doing anything wrong" you won't be sued. From a defensive perspective, having a patent portfolio gives a startup bargaining chips to play in the event that it is sued for infringement; no portfolio leaves few options and even less leverage.

Our product/service doesn't contain any patentable inventions

Identification of IP is something that many people struggle with, and we will address that issue in more depth later. But suffice it to say that if you have technology (hardware, software, etc.) that provides competitive advantage, it is likely you have IP. We highly recommend that you use an invention discovery tool or speak to a patent professional to help tease out any valuable IP you may have.

3

WHAT EXACTLY IS A PATENT?

A patent is a 20-year government-granted monopoly for an invention. It gives your company a competitive advantage in the marketplace.

In the United States, a patent (from the filing date of the non-provisional application) is a 20-year government-granted monopoly for an invention, which generally speaking is a product or a process that provides, a new way of doing something or offers a new technical solution to a problem. One very important distinction that many people do not understand is that a patent does not directly give your company the right to ship your product. Rather, a patent potentially allows you to stop someone else from shipping their product. If you have evidence that another company, without your agreement, is making, using, or selling your invention in the same country that awarded your patent, you can then ask the courts to stop it from doing so.

The U.S. is now a "First-to-File" nation, meaning that the right to the patent for a given invention belongs to the first person to file a patent application for said invention.

A First-to-File system increases the urgency with which inventors should act upon protecting their intellectual property.

As a result of this urgency, **it's often wise for businesses to file provisional patent applications** prior to converting them to non-provisional patents.

A few reasons why this is a smart move:

- Provisional patent applications are lower cost than non-provisional applications
- Provisional patent applications are faster/easier to produce/file than non-provisional applications
- Provisional patent applications buy you 12 months of "patent pending" protection status, during which you can hone and perfect your idea before deciding to pursue a more expensive, time-consuming non-provisional patent application. (Before that 12 month deadline, you must either convert the provisional application into a non-provisional patent application, re-file the provisional application which resets the priority date, or abandon the idea).

What is in a patent application document?

A patent is constructed in three sections: the claims, the figures, and the description. The most important of the three sections is the claims. We say this for two reasons:

First, the claims comprise the legal description of the invention and therefore dictate the actual boundaries of your intellectual property ownership. The rest of the patent is simply there to support the claims.

Second, most CEOs read a part of a patent description,

such as the summary or abstract, and believe they understand the legally protected invention. Most often they do not. Summaries and abstracts can sound really good (much better than the inventive claims warrant), when in reality the summary and abstract may not accurately convey what is protected.

Anatomy of a Patent

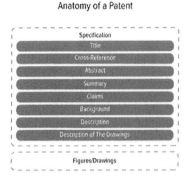

There are two types of patents:

- **Utility** patents are the most common type of patent filed. Utility patents protect functional aspects of an invention.
- **Design** patents protect the appearance or ornamental design of an invention.

Beyond patents, there are other forms of intellectual property that are worth briefly mentioning:

- A **trade secret** is information that gives a business a commercial advantage in the marketplace and is the subject of reasonable efforts to keep it a secret. Unlike a patent, a trade secret requires no registration and has no expiration date. (One of the world's most famous trade secrets is the formula for making Coca-Cola, which has remained a tightly held secret for more than 125 years.) To qualify as a trade secret, the invention must conform to three rules: (1) it cannot be generally known to the public; (2) it must have economic value derived from being kept secret; and (3) the company must make efforts to maintain the secrecy of the invention. The most straightforward way to create a trade secret is to draft a patent application but not file it with the USPTO. Instead, mark the application "Confidential/Trade Secret" and then protect and monitor access to it. Just as your employees and contractors sign IP assignment rights transfer agreements for relevant inventions, those who have access to trade secrets should acknowledge the importance and confidentiality of the company's trade secrets.
- A **copyright** grants the creator of an original work exclusive rights for its use and distribution for a limited amount of time.
- A **trademark** is a distinguishable design that distinguishes products or services of a particular company from others. Unlike other forms of IP, trademark rights are typically derived from the use of a specific design.

Note: For the purposes of this document, we won't go into great detail on copyrights and trademarks, but a brief chat with a legal professional can help you determine if a copyright or trademark is a worthwhile path for a business to pursue.

4

HOW DO WE KNOW IF WE HAVE A PATENTABLE IDEA?

At the most basic level, an invention must fulfill the following requirements to be considered for a patent:

1. The subject matter must be **patent-eligible.** Section 101 of the U.S. Patent Act, found in Title 35 of the United States Code, states that "Whoever invents or discovers any new and useful process, machine, manufacture, or composition of matter, or any new and useful improvement thereof, may obtain a patent therefor, subject to the conditions and requirements of this title."

2. The invention must be **new or novel.** If an invention was known to the public prior to an inventor filing a patent application, the invention cannot be considered new or novel, and is therefore not patentable. In other words, a patent cannot be granted if it prevents people from doing what they had previously been free to do. This requirement for novelty exists to ensure that

existing inventions, also known as prior art, are not patented again. All information relevant to a patent's claims of novelty that has been disclosed to the public, no matter the form in which it was presented, is considered prior art.

3. An invention must be **non-obvious**. This means that an invention must be a non-obvious improvement over existing products or practices. If it is deemed that an invention could easily be discovered by someone of "ordinary knowledge" or follow from "normal development" in a given field, the invention is not patentable. Additionally, if the invention is simply a routine or predictable combination or application of existing technology, it is not patentable.

4. An invention must be **useful**, meaning that the USPTO's patent examiners must determine that an invention has a specific utility.

Patentability

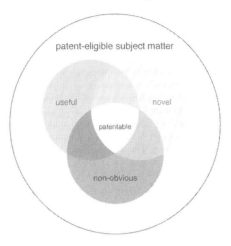

Now knowing what it takes for an idea to be patentable, we will assume that your solution is useful. Why else would you be creating it? We will focus the patentable invention investigation on patent-eligible, novel, and non-obvious to determine if your technology or processes contain inventive material.

Generally, when reviewing your product and roadmap for patentable inventions, you should focus on your most significant differentiators and competitive advantages. What do you want your sales and marketing people to tell potential clients? Is your company's solution faster, cheaper, smaller, easier to use, etc.? How did you make it so or how do you plan to make it so?

When trying to determine where in your technology there may be good IP, often an engineering team is unaware that what they have created is novel and non-obvious. It's been our ongoing experience that talented engineering staffs frequently dismiss the possibility of their creation being patentable. This is an area where automation can really help.

Automated invention discovery tools can compare product information to a vast database of prior art and help give you an idea of whether or not patentable material exists within your solution. It can also be helpful to have a patent expert examine your technical material and/or hold a brief invention investigative session with your key engineers. It is best to do this prior to publicly disclosing your innovations or offering for sale products that contain your innovations.

Going forward, have your engineering team document new projects, upgrades, and designs in enough detail to have someone of a similar skill level be able to reconstruct it without too much experimentation. This enhances future invention disclosures and will provide a ready-made basis for your next set of provisional patent applications.

HOW DOES MY COMPANY OBTAIN A PATENT?

Patent Filing Process

Your provisional patent application allows you to file a "mini" version of a patent application at a point where you may not have all the kinks worked out. This lets your company lay claim to your inventions as soon as possible, giving you an early priority date while you continue to develop the idea. You then have up to 12 months to decide whether or not to file the full (non-provisional) patent application, and incorporate any intervening developments into the non-provisional application, all while retaining the early priority date.

A provisional application will not be reviewed by the

government patent examiner until after the non-provisional application is filed, at which point it is important that a provisional application has enough detail to allow the examiner to determine that the information disclosed in the provisional application supports what is disclosed in the non-provisional application. It is extremely important to have a high quality provisional application drafted and filed. Amateur efforts in this process can cause more problems than benefits.

After a non-provisional application is filed, the application will be assigned to an art unit (a small division of the patent office which examines applications on related subject matter). Using an accelerated process (Track One), a response can come very quickly and a patent may be granted in less than a year. Think FedEx for patent applications. The standard application process typically takes approximately 20 months before it lands on an examiner's desk, and another year or so to process the patent application.

The examiner's job is essentially to test your patent application and find some reason to reject it. The examiner does this by comparing your patent application to the technical rules on patent drafting as well as comparing it to previously published patent specifications and public literature (referred to as "prior art").

Once an examiner completes an examination he or she most often issues a rejection and the inventor or the inventor's representative (a patent professional) must respond to the rejection through what is known as an **office action** and **office action response.**

An office action is a formal written correspondence from the patent examiner containing the issues he or she has with your application. Your company's representative will read the examiner's remarks and make arguments about the application's patentability or suggest amendments to the patent application to address the basis for the examiner's rejection.

While the rejection rate can vary widely between art units and examiners, it is not uncommon for an application to undergo three or more cycles of exchanges with the patent office before a patent application is granted an allowance or a company gives up and abandons the effort. In the event that the application is allowed, the company pays a fee to obtain the final granted patent.

Once granted, the final patent is published, listing the inventors and/or your corporate entity as the owner of this intellectual property.

Congratulations! Your company now has the first granted asset in your patent portfolio.

HOW LONG DOES IT TAKE TO OBTAIN A PATENT?

AND HOW MUCH DOES IT COST?

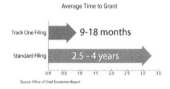

Average Time to Grant

One of the biggest questions people have about the patent process is about how long it takes, most often in reference to both the application process and the amount of time the inventor must spend away from daily tasks.

The standard patent process itself takes an average of more than three years. However, an increasing number of companies are beginning to use what is known as the Track One accelerated process. This faster process guarantees a response from the USPTO within one year and final resolution within eighteen months.

Track One costs small corporations an additional $2,000 upfront per patent application. While the upfront cost is higher, we've found (as have others who have analyzed the process) that the total cost can be the same or even less than for non-accelerated applications. Additionally, the grant rate is consistently and significantly higher for Track One applications.

The inventor-time typically required as part of the patent process can vary widely depending on the invention. When the invention disclosure is created as part of the engineering process, it maximizes the efficiency of the creation of IP and creates higher quality results.

How much does a patent cost?

Patent Costs[†]

Type of Application	Examples	Traditional Cost	AIP Cost
Provisional	all	$3,000- $5,000	$1,500-$2,000
Simple	paper clip, board game	$5,000- $10,000	$3,000-$5,000
Moderately Complex	power tool, cell phone	$8,000- $12,000	$4,000-$6,000
Highly Complex / Software	MRI scanner, automated system	$12,000- $15,000	$6,000-$8,000

[†] based on small entity filing
http://www.ipwatchdog.com/2015/04/04/the-cost-of-obtaining-a-patent-in-the-us/id=56485/
http://www.blueironip.com/what-do-patents-actually-cost/

If you ask most law firms how much you can expect to pay for a patent, the answer you'll likely get is "it depends." It's a fair answer, but not a particularly useful one. The fact is that law firms typically charge anywhere between $3,000 to $15,000 to file a provisional patent application or non-provisional patent application, depending on how complex the invention is and how much the firm charges per hour.

Patent firm alternatives (such as the one offered by my company, TurboPatent) have a staff of trained patent engineers who utilize AI and machine learning (Automated Invention Protection, or AIP) to create high quality patents in less time and therefore at a lower cost. In many cases, an AIP-powered patent filing costs 50 to 60% less than a manual one.

7

WHAT ARE THE BEST PATENT PRACTICES FOR EARLY STAGE COMPANIES?

Best practices start with the executive team modeling a behavior demonstrating the importance of protecting the company's inventions with patents or trade secrets from the outset of the conception and planning of your products and services. We call this "Inventioneering." Great leadership teams and their companies (such as Apple, Google, Amazon, and Microsoft, to name a few), take IP very seriously. You should too, and with Inventioneering you can exceed the IP practices of each of these companies.

Summary of Best Practices

- Understand your company's motivations for protecting IP.
- Leaders regularly message these motivations to the company.
- Legal review of employee/contractor agreements.
- NDAs for interviews, partnerships, and other discussions.

- Capture inventive concepts at the outset of product and roadmap planning.
- Set regular (monthly or quarterly) meetings purposely targeted at identifying and capturing IP.
- Executives attend IP meetings, both to emphasize their importance and to offer their own contributions. The best CEOs are also inventors.
- Use technology to identify and capture invention and create appropriate documents.
- Engage a patent professional with appropriate experience and domain expertise. Request proof and references. Make sure you're not getting into a "bait and switch" scenario. Use technology to evaluate patent document drafts.
- Begin with a provisional patent application. Make sure it is adequately reviewed by inventor(s) prior to submission. Be sure to get assignment from all inventors at the point of each filing. Prioritize the production of a comprehensive, quality application. First to File wins the race!
- Convert provisional patent applications to non-provisional applications well ahead of the 12-month deadline. Determine Track One or standard process depending upon company goal. File a broad specification and narrow claims. Review to make sure claims faithfully capture the invention. Check the box to keep your filing confidential throughout the examination process (unless you intend to file outside of the U.S.).
- Stay involved during examination, making sure important claims do not drift away from

company goals. Use technology to help monitor claims throughout the examination process.

- File a continuation before or after allowance (but a must-file before grant!). Always keep a continuation open on each family.
- Utilize an employee recognition program. Recognition awards are typically more effective than cash awards.

Understand your company's motivations for protecting IP

We know that early-stage companies typically face tough budgetary and time constraints. It's difficult for a startup CEO to choose between spending more money on developing a product or service and legally protecting the innovations encapsulated in those products. So before you start down the patent path, have a really good grasp on why you and your company are doing so. We covered 11 good reasons to pursue the protection of your company's IP earlier in this document, but there may also be others. While there is not a single motive for all companies, having worked with hundreds of startups, we can say there are several common reasons shared by entrepreneurs pursuing patents, including:

- Defense against copycats and fast followers
- Improving odds of getting VC or strategic funding
- Improving valuation of funding or exit
- Demonstration of management professionalism and discipline
- Using the process to clearly understand

differentiation for product development and market development purposes
- Establishing "Patent Pending" or "Patented" for marketing purposes
- Enhancing employee (inventor) morale
- Freedom to disclose and have deeper discussions with other parties, especially those unable or unwilling to sign NDAs

Leaders continuously message these motivations to the company

Best patent practices start at the top of the organization. If the CEO consistently communicates the importance of protecting the company's intellectual assets, then it becomes part of the culture and priorities of the company.

Legal review of employee/contractor agreements

It is critical that each employee and contractor sign an agreement that makes it clear that any intellectual property that is related to the company business or created using company time and/or equipment is the property of the company. By law, inventions are 100% owned by each inventor. If even one inventor does not assign the invention to the company, then the company does not have sole ownership of the IP.

NDAs for interviews, partnerships and other discussion

Non-disclosure agreements (NDAs) should be signed by every employee, contractor, vendor who has knowledge of the company's IP, interviewee who will see proprietary inventive material during the hiring process, and anyone having a discussion with the company regarding its IP. NDAs are not a substitute for having patents filed on your inventions, but they are better than having no protection. It is also the case that larger companies will insist that you sign their NDA. The problem, however, is that many of these NDAs have clauses (see *residual clause*) that make them very weak when it comes to protecting IP.

One of the primary needs of a startup or small business is to secure funding, often in the form of meeting with venture capitalists to present the business's core ideas and differentiators. In a perfect world, a startup CEO would be able to count on the protection of an NDA for these kinds of meetings, but the fact is that most potential investors won't sign them, leaving the startup disclosing its "secret sauce" without any protection. Filing patents on core ideas prior to disclosing ideas to potential investors allows the savvy startup CEO to protect the value of the company proactively, without relying on VCs to keep the startup's plans under wraps.

Capture inventive concepts at the outset of product and roadmap planning

The time to capture the patentable concepts is at the very beginning of the productization process. Waiting until a week before launching the product produces bad results.

The patenting process can help startups develop a superior product and better value proposition. Because the patent process requires engineering and management teams to introspect about their products/services, the exercise of writing a patent often reveals a company's strongest value proposition. Patents can also help motivate team members, whether through an increased sense of ownership in the product, a feeling of accomplishment, or incentive-based competitions (more on this later).

Set regular (monthly or quarterly) meetings purposely targeted at identifying and capturing IP

Consistent with building invention protection into your culture, you should take a bit of time on a regular basis to inspect your products and roadmaps for patentable material. You should also encourage the team to think out several years to imagine the path and intersection of the industry and your roadmap. Some of your very best IP will be for products or features that will not arrive for several years.

Executives attend meetings, both to emphasize their importance and to offer their own contributions. The best CEOs are also inventors.

Members of the management team, especially the CEO, should attend as many of the invention brainstorming sessions as possible, which reinforces the importance of invention to the company. It should also be noted that the best tech CEOs have been inventors: Steve Jobs, Bill Gates, Paul Allen, Elon Musk, Jeff Bezos, Mark Zuckerberg, Larry Page, Sergey Brin—the list goes on.All are inventors who attended such meetings.

Use technology to identify and capture invention and create appropriate documents

One frequent question we hear is "How do we know if we have a patentable invention?" AI technology exists that allows a product team to drop a product spec or description into a system that will then provide guidance on the patentability of the technology. Additionally, this technology can help the team extract the inventive concepts in more detail to facilitate a faithful capture of the true and intended invention. Available products include Idea Journaling, Invention Discovery, Invention Capture, and the automation of the preparation and prosecution of patent applications.

Engage a patent professional with appropriate experience and domain expertise. Request proof and references. Make sure you're not getting into a "bait and switch" scenario. Use technology to evaluate patent document drafts.

It is a frequent practice of large law firms to have inexperienced associates work on the patent matters of smaller entities. Quite bluntly, your business is not critical to the larger firm so they use your material as training fodder for their junior people.And although patent professionals require a technology degree to become certified by the US Patent and Trademark Office (USPTO), any registered patent professional can practice in any domain, which means someone with a Bachelor of Science degree in biology could be assigned to write a patent on your machine learning breakthrough—a clear domain mismatch. The lesson here: make sure the person helping you has deep experience in your subject matter. Finally, in addition to the fact that the best professionals will proactively show proof of the quality of their work, there are also AI tools that can automatically evaluate the technical proficiency of previous applications written by the person in charge of your case.

Begin with provisional patent application. Make sure it is adequately reviewed by inventors(s) prior to submission. Be sure to get assignment from all inventors at the point of each filing. Prioritize the production of a comprehensive, quality application. First to File wins the race!

As of 2013, the United States is a "first-to-file" nation. That means the first person or entity to file a patent application on the inventive material has priority over anyone else who attempts to file after that. Therefore, it is very important to get your inventions filed as applications as soon as possible. Because it is faster and cheaper to file a provisional application, do that first.

Once you've filed, you can refer to your invention as "PATENT PENDING." Also, by going the provisional route you add up to a year of additional protection (for a total of up to 21 years) for your invention. The provisional patent application gives you up to 12 months to file the non-provisional application. While speed is one of the goals of the provisional filing, it's critical to do a complete job in describing your invention in this application. Claims and drawings are not required for a provisional filing but they are highly recommended. Not recommended: "skinny provisionals," which contain little description and no claims or drawings; they are, in fact, a bad idea.

If your provisional does not fully describe your invention then you will not be allowed to claim the priority date. Worse yet, you may not discover this until your patent is tested in the courts via litigation, sale of your patent, or some other event that occurs after the patent has been granted. The more descriptive and complete the provisional, the better served you will be in supporting the conversion to the non-provisional. At this point you should have each inventor named on the application sign an assignment agreement. I know their employment or contractor documents indicate that their inventions are owned by the company, but do it anyway. "Belts and suspenders!" Disputes of patent ownership are way too common to take any chances.

Convert provisional patent applications to non-provisional applications well ahead of the 12-month deadline. Determine Track One or standard process depending upon company goal. File a broad specification and narrow claims. Review to make sure claims faithfully capture the invention. Check the box to keep your filing confidential throughout the examination process (unless you intend to file outside of the U.S.).

Target to convert your provisional to a non-provisional around the six- to eight-month time frame, or even sooner. Bad things can easily happen when you are fighting a deadline. Depending upon your strategy, determine if filing Track One is right for your situation. Track One patent applications have a high allowance rate and are granted with fewer office actions. In general, you get better results with Track One, and our overall experience is that it is cheaper in the long run, even though it costs $2,000 more to start with. This is true because there is less back and forth with the patent office, resulting in lower overall prosecution costs.

Make sure the inventors have engaged in a meaningful review of the application. If you are patenting something other than what your team intended, then you have protected something that has little or even no relevance to your business goals. This is one of the biggest problems we run across in the patent industry. Straying from a faithful representation of the invention happens when the inventors are too busy or too important to be bothered, leaving the practitioner (most often someone minimal domain expertise) to rely on his or her own creative juices to put something down on paper.

There is a filing option (a box to check) that allows you to keep your application from being published until it is allowed as a granted patent. If the USPTO denies your application, it is never made public.

It's also time to have all the inventors sign another assignment agreement.

Stay involved during examination, making sure important claims do not drift away from company goals. Use technology to help monitor throughout the examination process.

The next step is to receive an office action from the patent office. This will happen within months under the Track One scenario and in about two years using the standard path. It is most common that the examiner will find some rationale to test your application with what is known as a rejection (and which usually turns out to be multiple rejections).

Your practitioner will need to respond to these rejections with well thought out arguments. This is a point where the intended claims of your invention can "drift" or "rot." Once again, if your inventors are not engaged properly, the practitioner will do his or her the best to respond, often in a way that goes astray of the true invention. In large companies this dysfunction is more common than not. If you pay attention, this is where your smaller company has an advantage.

File a continuation before or after allowance (but a must-file before grant!). Always keep a continuation open on each family.

This is an advanced and nuanced part of patent strategy, but very powerful. With the provisional you wrote a broad specification with many drawings. You converted that into the non-provisional, adding material that was consistent with the material described in the provisional so you have good support for our priority date granted by the provisional application.

Now for the advanced stuff. You file a very narrow set of claims describing very specifically the invention contained in the improvement to your product. This narrow claim set allows for a more efficient examination process, lowering the cost and time of prosecution. Good enough; you rapidly get an allowance from your examiner establishing a relationship and positive precedent.

Part of the patent process allows for filing more claims against the non-provisional application as long as the new claims are supported in the specification of the original patent application. This is known as a "continuation."

You can file a continuation any time prior to paying the grant fees on the previous application. It can even be years later. This future claiming process allows you to observe what has happened in the market and with your competitor's products and then steer the new claims towards those products. The claims must be supported from the original broad specification but can also take advantage of the knowledge gleaned from years of industry progress —all while still enjoying the filing date of the original provisional application. It's like being able to jump into a time machine!

Utilize an employee recognition program. Recognition awards are typically more effective than cash awards.

Employee patent reward and recognition programs work! That said, it's my observation that the recognition part works more than the reward part.

Some companies give cash bonuses for inventor contributions. A set amount split among the inventors of a provisional, with more money for a non-provisional and even more for a granted patent. Other tech companies give inventors something to display on their desk or in their office. I have seen stackable engraved acetate blocks (such as the one pictured below) proudly displayed by brilliant engineers.

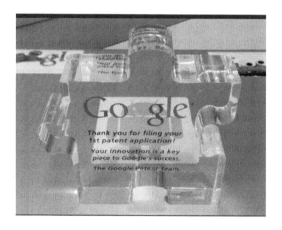

8

WHAT ABOUT FILING FOR PROTECTION IN COUNTRIES OUTSIDE THE U.S.?

Without going into too much detail, it's safe to say that international patent filings are expensive and time-consuming.

Below is a simple timeline of the process (note: not to scale) to give you a sense of how long a global patent filing typically takes:

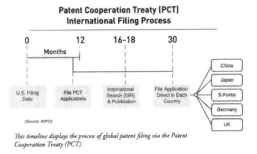

This timeline displays the process of global patent filing via the Patent Cooperation Treaty (PCT).

The bottom line is that you have **12 months after filing for patent protection in the United States to file under the Patent Cooperation Treaty (PCT), which preserves your**

right to file in any of the 148 countries participating in the PCT.

The cost to file with the PCT is $2,500. However, the eventual cost of filing in the separate countries varies. Here is a list of the most important jurisdictions among the countries, which represent about 80% of all patent applications and grants worldwide.

International Patent Costs

Jurisdiction	Cost in US Dollars
+Patent Cooperation Treaty (PCT)	$2,500
China	$25,000
Japan	$25,000
S. Korea	$25,000
Germany	$20,000
UK	$7,500
Total	**$105,000**

(Source: www.WIPO.int)

Energy is a function of mass and speed. As a startup, your company enjoys neither the benefit of large piles of cash nor huge numbers of employees and other resources. But you can compensate for your lack of size by moving quickly to generate market energy. It's also true that with the momentum that large companies achieve through their market successes brings inertia.

Your smaller company can more easily and quickly create and implement innovative solutions than can lumbering giants. I suspect that the above statements are not surprising, as it's been long taught that smaller organizations have the ability to move faster, are less thought-constrained, and can implement more quickly than large, established corporations.

What may come as a surprise is that early-stage companies also have the ability to protect their inventions faster, cheaper, and better than large organizations.

Faster: In most of the world, including the United States, the first inventor to file an application for an invention is the owner of that invention. Large corporations have long invention discovery, disclosure, and approval processes. And once approved for drafting, the bespoke approaches they employ to draft and file a patent application usually take months.

In a typical large company, it's very common for six months or more to pass from the point an inventive concept is uncovered to the point of filing with the USPTO.

Using the Inventioneering approach of combining the discovery of your company's invention immediately upon the creation of the product with the use of automated invention protection (AIP), an early-stage company can go from invention discovery to filing in a month or less. But you must not hesitate, as your time advantage will evaporate quickly.

Cheaper: The United States Patent Office gives "small entities" (companies with fewer than 500 employees) a 50% discount on fees associated with filing and prosecuting a patent. Additionally, large companies tend to be encumbered by legacy relationships with inefficient, high-overhead law firms. Both large companies and the patent firms they use are slow to adopt automation technology that reduces cost.

The high costs surrounding the traditional patenting process is what most often causes CEOs of a startup companies to hesitate. He or she is often faced with the false choice of "Do I spend my limited capital on building the product or do I address the legalities of protecting my crown jewels"?

Luckily, there are new ways to reduce the drafting and prosecution costs without sacrificing quality. In fact, the quality inherent in these options will more than likely be superior. Combining the patent process with engineering, an approach that includes automation and analytic technologies, can reduce your overall costs by 50% or more. This is true for two reasons:

First, the automation tools allow the patent professional to create high quality patent documents in a fraction of the time as compared to traditional methods. Second, the engineering approach uses huge data sets to analyze and deliver documents that flow more easily through the examination process. "Greasing the skids" at the USPTO decreases the time and energy required to obtain a granted patent, thereby significantly decreasing the cost.

Better: Being able to execute faster and cheaper than a large organization can is a straightforward and obvious advantage. Understanding how and why your organization can obtain better IP requires two things: first, you should know how dysfunctional the patent process often is in large organizations, and second, you need to learn how NOT to let your organization fall into traps that result from those dysfunctions.

A large company will have a portfolio containing thousands of patents. IBM, for example, maintains about 40,000 U.S. patents; the company plays a quantity game. It's an outdated strategy but large organizations change very slowly. In fact, it's likely that the vast majority of many companies' patents are invalid, unenforceable, or worthless for other reasons. This occurs because a large company's dedicated patent organization is focused on filing and "successfully" prosecuting a specific number of patents every year. The engineers, scientists, and other inventors usually do not share that goal.

The result is that the inventors do not deeply engage in

the process. As a result, the invention that is prosecuted to allowance by the USPTO does not do a great job of faithfully representing an inventor's often brilliant idea.

Remember the game of telephone, where each time a message was transmitted to another person it degraded to the point where it became unrecognizable? Or the famous cartoon of a tree swing design that depicts the contrast between what the customer wanted and the ridiculously complex results delivered.

Well, in large companies—and too often in smaller companies as well—this is what happens during the patent process.

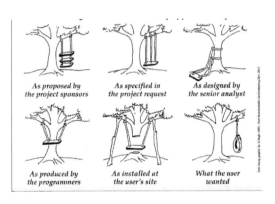

9

INVENTIONEERING

The process diagramed below occurs thousands of times each day throughout the world. The output of this work is usually one or more of the following: a PowerPoint deck, a product specification, system diagrams, flowcharts, CAD drawings, and maybe even a prototype.

All of these outputs are communication instruments used to create a common understanding among the stakeholders to the Inventioneering process including engineers, designers, marketers, salespeople, manufacturing workers, and executives.

A subsequent patent application is, in fact, simply another form of the same information. Most often a patent application can and should be created and filed far faster than the actual product can be built. Using a patent machine, an inventor can input the same information he or she is already creating in the engineering and development process—but now that information is used to produce a rough draft of a provisional patent. That draft provisional patent can then be rapidly reviewed and, once approved by your company, quickly completed and filed.

The below chart shows the ordered progression resulting in the creation of invention. Additionally, the same techniques used to identify worthy problems and novel solutions for the purposes of building products also can be used to anticipate future problems and predict future technologies that will allow for the creation of valuable IP.

These activities can be summarized as:
Problem, Idea, Innovation, Invention

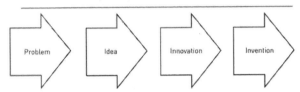

This charts the ordered progression resulting in the creation of invention.

In non-Inventioneering cultures, inventors often see the patent process as a nuisance getting in the way of their "real" jobs. As a result, their invention disclosures are anywhere from nonexistent to woefully incomplete. Requests for more and better information fall on deaf ears, leaving the person responsible for drafting an application to his or her own inventiveness. In these conditions, patent quality inevitably suffers. Even the best patent practitioners are not mind readers.

With Inventioneering and the use of a patent machine, these problems are eliminated at this phase of the process. The inventor uses an invention-capture system that is synergistic with his or her daily work efforts. The patent machine delivers for review a well-written and carefully illustrated draft of a provisional, along with an invention summary report containing analytical decision support metrics.

The Invention Summary Report (see below) uses

massive amounts of data from the USPTO and other sources to analyze the submission and provide pertinent predictions on such things as abstraction risk, novelty, and obviousness, as well as the likely assignment of the USPTO Art Unit and important associated statistics for that Art Unit.

Tools and Technologies

The Patent Machine

Patents are, by definition, highly structured documents that must follow a fixed set of rules published by the patent office. Thus, the automation of patenting is a bounded, structured, and proven to be a tractable technical problem. The result is that utilizing patent automation saves both time and money. The good news is that it also yields superior results.

Using the latest techniques in NLP, machine learning, and data analytics, so-called patent machines are already automating many of the tasks required in the drafting, prosecution, and assessment of intellectual property. The output of this computer-automated patenting approach is faster, cheaper, and of higher quality than that of even the most seasoned and efficient patent practitioners.

In short, a human patent master will never beat the patent machine; in fact, over time, the performance gap will only increase.

You would not hire a software developer who did not know how to use GitHub or a modern IDE. Similarly, you would not hire a designer or engineer who could not use the profession's power tools. So why would you hire a patent professional who employs Microsoft Word as be all end all of automation?

PATENT PHD FOR EARLY STAGE CEOS: FURTHER READING

Below is a collection of resources we've curated for those of you looking to further your patent knowledge:

- *Inventioneering* by James Billmaier & Britt Griffith
- *Provisional Patent Applications*, *Litigation-Proof Patents*, *True Patent Value*, and *Patent Portfolios*, by Larry Goldstein
- *Patents Demystified* by Dylan Adams
- *Investing in Patents* by Russ Krajec
- United States Patent & Trademark Office
- World Intellectual Propery Organization
- IP WatchDog Blog
- IP Strategies for Startups
- Waiting to Protect your IP Could Doom Your Startup

ABOUT THE AUTHOR

James Billmaier is the inventor of more than 100 patents and patent filings. He is the co-founder and CEO of Turbo-Patent Corporation and the co-author of *Inventioneering: The smartest CEOs will fuse engineering and invention to dominate the next decade.* James has previously served as chairman and CEO of three companies including Asymetrix, which he led to a successful IPO in 1998; Digeo, Inc., which he co-founded with Microsoft legend, Paul Allen,; and Melodeo, Inc., which was acquired by the Hewlett Packard Corporation in 2010. At Digeo, James became the only entrepreneur to ever win back-to-back EMMY awards for technical achievement. Under his leadership, he, Paul Allen, and the Digeo team filed more than 400 patents.

Contributors

Charles Mirho (BSEE, MSEE, JD), a co-founder of Turbo-Patent Corporation, has practiced patent law for more than 20 years. He was one of the first candidates selected for Intel's engineer-to-lawyer program in the early 1990s, and graduated at the top of his law school class with an intellectual property law specialty. Charles worked on developing Intel's Internet technology and software patent portfolio before moving on to private practice. Charles founded FSP LLC, a Northwest law firm specializing in patenting technologies in software, Internet, wireless, electronics, and communications.

Larry Goldstein (BA, Harvard; MBA, Northwestern; JD, University of Chicago) is an independent patent lawyer based in Tel Aviv, Israel, specializing in communications and computers. In addition to drafting applications and providing patent advice, he has written five books about patents—four of them as part of a series on patent quality—and a fifth about patent pools. He has served as a consulting witness in several major patent litigations on issues such as FRAND licensing, royalty rates, and the essentiality of patents to technical standards.

Joe Fortunato (JD) received his undergraduate degree from Washington State University and his Juris Doctor from Gonzaga University School of Law, where he focused his studies on Intellectual Property law and served as a Legal Fellow in the United States Congress. He is currently pursuing a degree in electrical engineering at the University of Washington Bothell, where he is a research assistant working on embedded systems development for biomedical applications.

Britt Griffith has always been passionate about invention, having earned her first granted patent at the age of 15. Britt graduated from Stanford University with bachelor's and master's degrees in digital media, where she received Academic All-American honors and graduated first in her graduate program. She was previously a contributing writer to the Pulitzer Prize-winning team at the *San Francisco Chronicle*, and is currently TurboPatent's director of marketing. Britt is the co-author of *Inventioneering*.

NEED A PATENT?

WE CAN HELP

TurboPatent has reinvented the patent process using AI and machine learning to both drive down the costs and increase the quality of patents.

Our U.S.-based patent experts operate TurboPatent's PatentBrain™ to deliver high quality applications and Office action responses at a fraction of the cost and turn-around time of traditional, human-centered practices.

Visit turbopatent.com for more information.

How We Can Help

- Free consultation
- Patent filing (provisional, non-provisional)
- Office action responses
- Invention discovery tools
- Invention discovery sessions
- Invention capture and management tools
- Automated quality assessments of current assets
- End-to-end processing of patents

DISCLAIMER

The provided information is for assisting with business strategy purposes only and does not constitute legal advice.

TurboPatent is not a law firm and is not providing legal advice. All information available in this document and associated references is provided without any warranty, express or implied, including as to their legal effect and completeness. The information should be used as a guide and modified to meet your company's own needs. Your use of any information is at your own risk. TurboPatent Corporation and any of its employees, contractors, advisors, or attorneys who participated in providing the information expressly disclaim any warranty: they are not creating or entering into any Attorney-Client relationship by providing information to you.